A-37/T-37 Dragonfly

in action

By Terry Love
Color By Don Greer
Illustrated by Joe Sewell

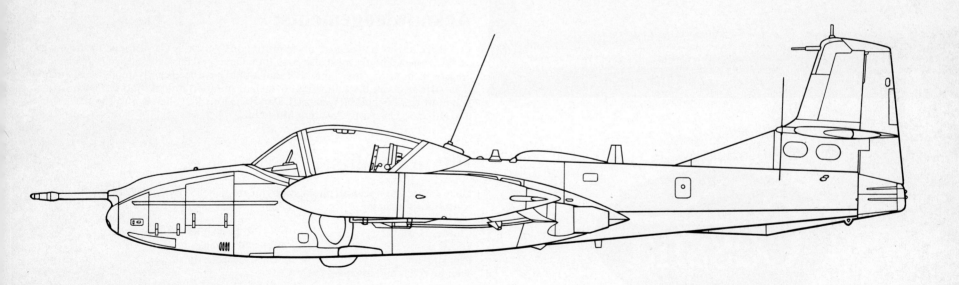

Aircraft Number 114
squadron/signal publications

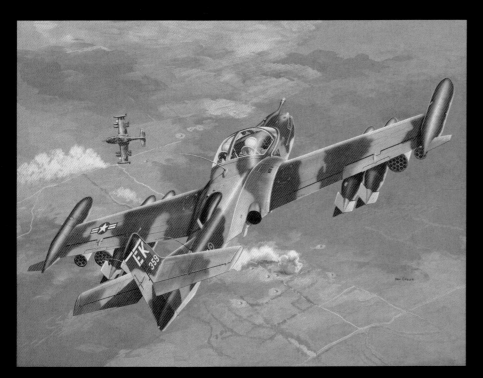

LT Tom O'Beirne of the 8th SOS, 14th SOW rolls in on a ground support mission over South Vietnam during 1970. The A-37B Dragonfly was used by both the USAF and Vietnamese Air Force (VNAF) for air support missions over the South.

ISBN 0-89747-239-X

If you have any photographs of the aircraft, armor, soldiers or ships of any nation, particularly wartime snapshots, why not share them with us and help make Squadron/Signal's books all the more interesting and complete in the future. Any photograph sent to us will be copied and the original returned. The donor will be fully credited for any photos used. Please send them to:

Squadron/Signal Publications, Inc.
1115 Crowley Drive.
Carrollton, TX 75011-5010.

Dedication:

To the late, great Mr. Robert J. Pickett of Cessna Aircraft. Friend, historian, and photographer — this is for you pal.

Acknowledgements:

I especially wish to express my appreciation to my wife, Carol, for all the time spent on this project. Thanks must also go to John Davis and the Wichita Aviation Historical Society; without their assistance this book would have been nearly impossible to write. I also wish to thank the following for their inspiration and assistance; Mike Langer, Wayne Mutza, Nicholas J. Waters III, Dan Hagedorn, Ben Sherels, and Thomas J. Sabiston, Director, U.S. Army Aviation Museum.

Photo Credits:

Unless otherwise noted, all photographs are from the Robert J. Pickett collection. Other contributors include:

Charles B. Mayer
USAF
Pete Harlem
Wichita Aviation Historical Society

Robert Chad LeBeau
Nick Waters
Dan Hagedorn

This Cessna T-37B (60-0131) of the Air Training Command carries early 1960s trainer markings consisting of an overall Natural Metal finish with Day Glo Orange nose, wing and tail panels.

Introduction

One of the more neglected areas of aviation history has been the history of training and light attack aircraft. Numerous aircraft, such as the T-6 and T-28, that were designed for pilot instruction were built with armament and were used as light attack aircraft. What makes the Cessna T/A-37 stand out from all the rest is that it is still the front line basic jet trainer for the USAF and numerous other foreign air forces. Additionally, there are plans to refurbish the aircraft to give it another twenty years of service.

The biggest factor to success in combat is quality training. This has been proven time and time again in the skies over Europe, Korea, Vietnam and the Persian Gulf — training is the key to victory. To start pilots out on the proper course in their training, the selection of a good basic trainer is of vital importance.

The Cessna Aircraft Company of Wichita, Kansas, has a well deserved reputation as a designer and builder of outstanding light aircraft for utility, transport, and observation. The company gained some military experience during the Second World War II when they built the Cessna UC-78 Bobcat and followed this aircraft with the Cessna L-19/O-1 Bird Dog series of light observation aircraft. When the Air Force issued its Requests For Proposals (RFPs) during the early 1950s for a basic jet trainer, Cessna responded.

The USAF issued the full specification for the TX (Trainer Experimental) project on 15 April 1952. Some of the requirements were: an empty weight of 4,000 pounds (in order to limit costs and complexity), an ability to perform twenty takeoffs and landings within a two hour period, handling characteristics matched to those of a modern jet fighter, a 35,000 foot ceiling, sufficient high altitude maneuverability for student orientation, a maximum traffic pattern speed of 113 knots and good low speed handling characteristics.

The specification also included performance goals, weight limitations, the number and positions of the crew, and other details regarding systems and equipment. Several items were not specified and left up to the builder, including the number and type of engines. The designers could use jet or turbo-prop engines, although it was understood that the USAF preferred a jet powered basic trainer. Cessna engineers studied a large variety of configurations and finally decided on a small light weight twin jet design.

Cessna submitted their proposal during June of 1952 and during January of 1953, Cessna was notified by the USAF that its design had won the TX trainer competition (from some fifteen designs submitted by eight manufacturers). The trainer would be the first aircraft designed specifically for the subsonic jet training role. The USAF particularly liked the side-by-side seating arrangement which allowed a close liaison between the student and instructor during the early stages of the training syllabus.

On 16 April 1954, the Air Force awarded Cessna a contract (Contract AF 33(600)23681) for three experimental prototypes of the Cessna Model 318 under the designation XT-37 (Serials 54-0716 to 0718). At the same time, a second contract (AF 33(600)26718) was awarded for a single static test aircraft (serial 54-2731). The design of the XT-37 was a challenge to Cessna engineers because of the high and low speed requirements and the aircraft weight limitations. No compromise was permitted on the basic flight characteristics because of the aircraft's training mission.

To ensure the basic soundness of the design, wind tunnel tests were conducted at Wichita State University (low speed tests), Cornell University (high speed tests) and at the vertical wind tunnel of Wright-Patterson Air Force Base in Dayton, Ohio (spin tests).

The XT-37 prototype Cessna Model 318 emerged as a twin engined, side-by-side cockpit, cantilever low wing monoplane with an all metal semi-monocoque fuselage.

The XT-37 incorporated all the latest equipment and design techniques of high performance jet aircraft. It was equipped with ejection seats, a jettisonable canopy, electric trim tabs on all control surfaces, and hydraulically activated speed brakes. A wide tread landing gear (fourteen feet) and a steerable nose wheel was utilized for maximum safety in landings and ground operations. The XT-37 cockpit included provisions for both day and night instrument flying, oxygen equipment, heating and ventilating systems. The aircraft's gross weight was 5,000 pounds.

The XT-37s were each powered by two 920 lbst Continental/Teledyne J-69 turbojet engines (a license built French Turbomeca Marbore engine) submerged in the wing roots to provide for a minimum of ducting and a short tail pipe. The wings, which are set at a dihedral of 3°, were built on twin aluminum spars with all metal, high lift slotted flaps inboard of the ailerons. The combination of a low wing loading and the high lift flaps enabled the XT-37 to operate satisfactorily from short runways during hot weather.

The instructor and student were seated under a jettisonable, clamshell canopy. Each was provided with individual controls and instruments, with the controls for the flaps, speed brakes, trim tabs, and radios being positioned and operated in the same manner as contemporary USAF combat aircraft. The ejection seats were effective only above 100 feet and 138 mph.

The XT-37s were relatively small and simple which contributed to the ease of maintenance. Special attention was given to maintenance factors to assure a high percentage of aircraft readiness and a minimum turn-around time. Maintenance accessibility to equipment, systems, and the aircraft structure was designed into the aircraft from the beginning to facilitate repair and maintenance, with more than 100 access panels and doors being incorporated into the aircraft.

The short landing gear eliminated the need for ground stands and ladders and all areas of the engine compartment were readily accessible from ground level. An experienced ground crew can remove and reinstall an engine in about thirty minutes. All major assemblies are interchangeable and replaceable for effective maintenance in the field.

The XT-37 (54-0716) on the ramp at the Cessna facility shortly before its first flight. The first prototype had a curved vertical fin fillet and narrow chord rudder.

Because of its low drag characteristics, the XT-37 was equipped with a hydraulically operated speed brake located below the fuselage just behind the nosewheel well. Also hydraulically activated and a unique feature on the XT-37 was the thrust deflectors that deflected the engine exhaust, permitting higher RPM settings during landings. When the deflectors were extended, effective thrust was reduced by some forty percent, slowing the aircraft on approach.

Retractable engine air inlet screens were incorporated in the forward portion of each engine nacelle and operated in conjunction with the landing gear. The screens are extended automatically over the inlet when the gear is down and locked. These screens are designed to prevent Foreign Object Damage (FOD) to the engines.

The XT-37 made its first flight on 12 October 1954 under the control of Cessna test pilot Bob Hagen. The flight lasted one hour and five minutes, with the prototype being followed by a USAF T-33 and a Cessna 310. Approximately 1,000 test flights were flown by the three prototypes and both Cessna and Air Force pilots flew the aircraft to evaluate the design. The tests revealed that XT-37 had a top speed of 393 mph at 35,000 feet (with half fuel), and a maximum range of 935 miles (with a thirty minute reserve). The single engine service ceiling (military power) was 19,200 feet, stall speed was 92 mph (flaps up) and 77 mph (flaps down), rate of climb was 3,000 feet per minute and service ceiling (half fuel) was 39,800 feet.

The number one prototype (54-0716) crashed on its 205th flight during a spin test. Flight testing was conducted at Wichita, Kansas Edwards AFB, California; and Wright-Patterson AFB, Ohio. The flight tests revealed that the aircraft required some modifications to improve its stall characteristics. These included a change to the wing tip design to give the aircraft a milder stall. An air scoop was added in front of the cockpit for cabin ventilation and the nose cone was revised. A long strake was added to each side of the nose to improve spin characteristics. The engine air intakes were revised and a rotating beacon was added to the top of the fuselage just behind the cockpit. A stall warning spoiler was added to create a disturbed air buffet which warns the pilot when stall speed is being approached. The landing lights were repositioned from the nose to the wing.

The biggest area of change was in the tail section. The tail was lengthened, the vertical fin area was increased, the rudder was lowered and the horizontal stabilizer was decreased in span. The dorsal fin was changed to a more angular configuration and enlarged, and a ventral fin was added and the tail cone was revised.

Other various configurations were tested on the XT-37 including wing slats, cameras mounted in the fuselage, spoilers on the wings, leading edge extensions, and vortex generators on the wings. These were not approved. After the Air Force completed all its tests, the aircraft was approved for production under the designation T-37A.

Tail Development

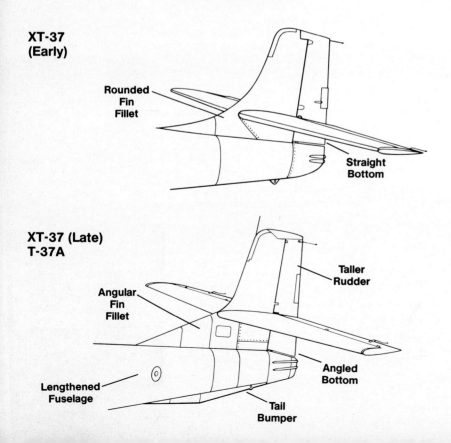

XT-37 (Early)
- Rounded Fin Fillet
- Straight Bottom

XT-37 (Late) T-37A
- Taller Rudder
- Angular Fin Fillet
- Angled Bottom
- Tail Bumper
- Lengthened Fuselage

The second XT-37 (54-0717) prototype featured a number of changes dictated by flight tests. The aircraft was modified with an angular fin fillet, lengthened fuselage, curved wing tip undersurfaces, wider chord rudder and tail bumper.

5

Development

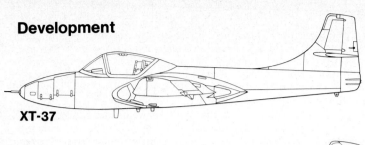

XT-37

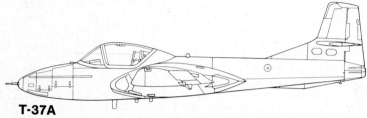

T-37A

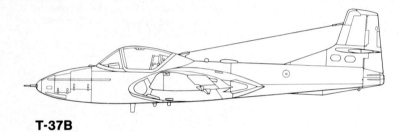

T-37B

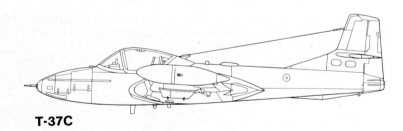

T-37C

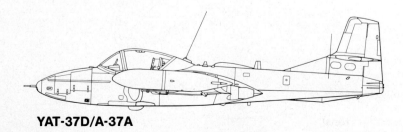

YAT-37D/A-37A

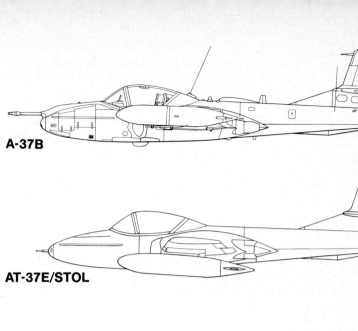

A-37B

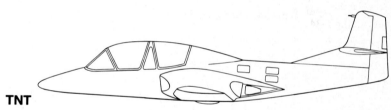

AT-37E/STOL

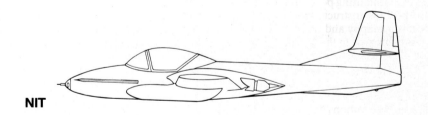

TNT

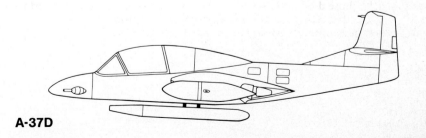

NIT

A-37D

T-37A

The production T-37A incorporated all the changes made to the XT-37 prototypes including the revised wing tip undersurface shape, cockpit ventilation air scoop, fuselage strake, enlarged engine air intakes, rotating beacon, lengthened fuselage, and revised tail section.

The production T-37A shared one feature that remained unchanged from the early XT-37 — the ear-piercing whine caused by the 21,730 rpm turbine blades of the J-69 engine. This sound earned the T-37 the nickname "The 6,000 pound dog whistle." From medium altitudes, the T-37 engine noise sounds like a fluttery whistle, which earned the aircraft its accepted nickname of "Tweety Bird" or just "Tweet."

The first production T-37A was completed on 3 September 1955, and made its acceptance flight on 27 September. After factory testing it was formally delivered to the Air Force during June of 1956.

T-37As began being used in test classes during 1957 where a number of student pilots were trained in the T-37A at Bainbridge Air Force Base, Georgia, under the *Project Pam* program, with Second Lieutenant Thomas W. Beaghen being the first student pilot to solo in a Cessna T-37A. During November of 1958 another student class started its flight training on the T-37A as part of *Project All-Jet*. The complete success of this program led to the retirement of the T-34 Mentor (the last USAF piston engined primary trainer) from the USAF training inventory on 1 April 1961. During 1965, the Air Force decided that a few hours in a Cessna T-41 piston engined trainer before transitioning to the T-37 would be more economical. The Air Force ordered a total of 444 T-37As, and the 200th aircraft rolled off the assembly line on 23 July 1958 with the last T-37A being produced during 1959.

The flight characteristics of the T-37A allowed students to solo after as little as six and a half hours of dual instruction. The aircraft's stability enabled it to be safely used for formation flying, yet the aircraft's power response was such that there remained a definite challenge in maintaining position throughout a formation flight. Most pilots who have flown the T-37 (as instructor pilots) compare it to a sports car. Although not overpowered, it is a snappy and responsive airplane that can do a loop within 2,500 feet of altitude (As compared to the T-38 Talon which requires 10,000 feet to complete a loop). All aerobatic maneuvers are permitted and easily performed.

On 29 May 1957, the U.S. Army began an evaluation program to investigate the possibilities of using the T-37A for photo reconnaissance, artillery observation, and other missions in support of ground forces. The program was called the High Performance Army Observation Aircraft or HPAOA. The tests involved three T-37As loaned to the Army and flown from the Army Aviation Center at Fort Rucker, Alabama. Seating arrangements, speed, and the general visual observation capabilities of the Cessna T-37A was similar to those desired by the Army; however, they desired a higher performance aircraft. The HPAOA program helped establish the Army requirement that eventually led to the development of the Grumman OV-1 Mohawk.

Air Force 56-3484 was an early production T-37A. The aircraft carried the Day Glo Red training color scheme used during the early 1960s. The instructor and student are both using P-4B flight helmets, which were being rapidly phased out at this time . (USAF)

Nose Development

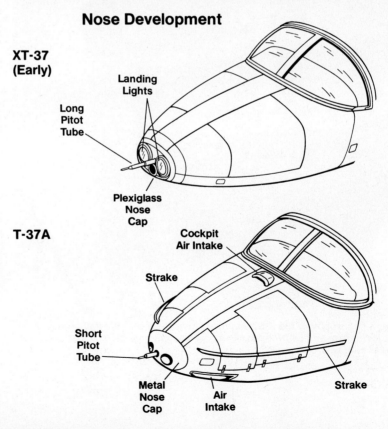

XT-37 (Early)

Long Pitot Tube
Landing Lights
Plexiglass Nose Cap

T-37A

Short Pitot Tube
Metal Nose Cap
Air Intake
Strake
Cockpit Air Intake
Strake

The basic design philosophy of the T-37 was that the side-by-side seating arrangement eased student instruction and allowed for close coordination between the instructor and student during all phases of training.

The first production T-37A (54-2729) was put on a flatbed trailer for transportation to the test site during September of 1955. The aircraft has not been modified with all the changes dictated by the flight tests since it was built before all of the test results were in.

The U.S. Army tested three Cessna T-37As during the Summer of 1957 under the High Performance Army Observation Aircraft program (HPAOA). The Army needed a higher performance aircraft for the observation role and eventually chose the Grumman OV-1 Mohawk.

A T-37 on final approach for landing. The wide track landing gear (14 feet) made landings in the T-37 easy for new pilots. Visibility from the cockpit was excellent through the large clam shell canopy.

This T-37A (54-2730) was the second T-37A built. The aircraft was on its acceptance flight over the flat Kansas prairie carrying an early USAF training scheme without Day Glo colors.

T-37B

The T-37B has evolved as the definitive variant of the T-37 basic jet trainer series and is, by far, the most common T-37 variant still in use. The T-37B differed from the earlier T-37A primarily in the power plants. To increase the aircraft's performance, the Air Force specified the use of the more powerful 1,025 lbst J-69-T-25 engine in place of the 920 lbst J-69-T-9 engine. The Air Force awarded Cessna a contract during early 1959 for the new T-37 and the first aircraft was delivered on 6 November 1959.

The first T-37B (Cessna model 318B) also featured improved communication and navigation equipment, including an improved UHF radio, OMNI navigational equipment and a revised instrument panel. The J-69-T-25 engines had increased reliability, improved performance, reduced operational costs, reduced maintenance requirements and a longer engine life. The new engines were approximately the same size as the earlier J-69-T-9 variant and required no external changes to the aircraft.

The J-69-T-25 engines had a fully automatic altitude compensating fuel control and drew fuel from the main fuselage tank immediately behind the cockpit. This tank is, in turn, fed from six inter-connected rubber fuel tanks in each wing. Engine-driven pumps and submerged booster pumps drive the automatic fuel transfer system, but in the event of a fuel system malfunction, fuel is automatically supplied to the engines by a gravity feed system.

As a result of damage sustained to the T-37 fleet during some 133 bird strikes (between 1965 and 1970), all T-37s have been retrofitted with a new windscreen made of Lexan polycarbonate plastic. This new windscreen is a half inch thick and is stressed to withstand the impact of a four pound bird at 288 mph.

Although the T-37B cockpit arrangement reproduces most of the characteristics of a modern combat aircraft, every effort has been made to achieve simplicity. The instrument panel is a relatively simple and straightforward approach to current requirements. The primary instruments are duplicated for both instructor and student. All instruments may be monitored and all operating controls and switches are easily accessible from either seat. Positioned to port on the student's side are the navigational and flight instruments, including directional and altitude indicators, altimeter, turn-and-bank, rate-of-climb, airspeed indicators and course indicators. In front of the instructor, on the starboard side (but within reach of the student) are the radio controls and circuit breakers. The engine instruments are mounted over the central panel and include tachometers, fuel flow, exhaust temperature indicators, fuel and oil pressure guages, load meters and an accelerometer. The control stick, grips and throttle quadrants are fighter type.

As a trainer, the T-37B demonstrates good stability in all configurations and flight conditions. The extremely effective control surfaces result in instant response and the balance between the three controls make maneuvers easily coordinated. Spins are mild and recovery is easily effected by using standard procedures. The aircraft has excellent stall characteristics, which are well defined. Stall warning is provided by a buffet in all flight configurations. Landings are accomplished equally well from either seat and there are no abrupt pitch or directional trim changes needed when power is added for a go-around.

Eventually all T-37As were returned to Cessna for conversion to T-37B standards. Between 1967 and 1968 additional contracts were awarded for continued production of the T-37B with deliveries running into 1973. A total of 552 new production T-37Bs were built.

This T-37B (60-0131) carries large "buzz" numbers, beginning with TE (the assigned T-37 code) on the fin in Black. The number consisted of TE and the last three digits of the aircraft's serial number.

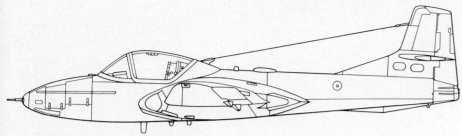

Specifications

Cessna T-37B

Wingspan .33 feet 9⅓ inches
Length . . . . .29 feet 3 inches
Height . . . . .9 feet 2 inches
Empty Weight . . . . .4,056 pounds
Maximum Weight . . . . .6,569 pounds
Powerplants . . . . .Two 1,025 lbst Continental
J-69-T-25 engines.

Armament . . . . .None

Performance
  Maximum Speed . . . . .425 mph
  Service ceiling . . . . .25,000 feet
  Range . . . . .932 miles
Crew . . . . .Two

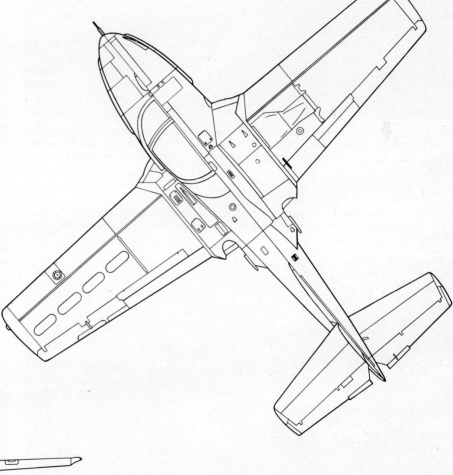

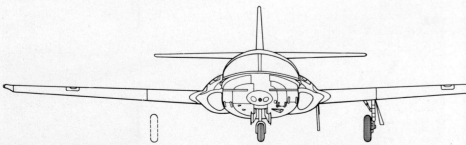

This T-37B (67-14745) was the 1,000th T-37 off the production line. The aircraft was delivered to the Air Training Command during 1967. The Red stripe across the fuselage was the turbine warning stripe, which revealed the location of the engine turbine section to ground crews.

This T-37B (60-0141) was assigned to ASD at Wright-Patterson AFB, Dayton, Ohio to flight test various items of equipment. The purpose of the cone-shaped device on the rudder is unknown, but it was probably connected with icing tests.

T-37B (60-0141) was later repainted in an overall White scheme with Red wing, nose, and fin bands. The special test nose probe carried Red and White stripes as a warning to ground personnel.

This T-37B (59-0376) was painted in Bi-Centennial markings during 1976. The nose was Red and White with a Blue anti-glare panel with White Stars. The canopy fairing was Blue with White Stars and the fin was Red, White and Blue with White Stars, while the tail bumper was also Blue with White stars.

This overall White T-37B was assigned to NASA at Edwards Air Force Base, California, during 1977 for various utility missions. The aircraft retained USAF markings along with the Yellow and Black NASA fin markings.

A T-37B (58-1864) of the 65th Flight Training Wing (FTW) at Reese Air Force Base. The aircraft was originally built as a T-37A and was later rebuilt to T-37B standards. The *Reese 01* marking on the fin identifies the aircraft as the wing commander's personal mount.

A T-37B on the ramp at Offut Air Force Base in the trainer markings carried during the 1980s. The new scheme consisted of Gloss White uppersurfaces over Dark Blue undersurfaces with Red lettering. (Author)

This Gloss White and Dark Blue T-37B carries a Blue and White checkerboard on the fin and has an Air Force Outstanding Unit award ribbon on the fin under the aircraft serial number. The small triangle under the cockpit is the Red ejection seat warning.

13

T-37C

U.S. Air Force interest in counterinsurgency (COIN) operations began during the early 1960s under President Kennedy. For COIN operations the Air Force needed a light, low cost combat aircraft that could be easily maintained in the field. Various armed trainers were evaluated including armed T-6G and T-28s, and at one point the Air Force even evaluated bringing back the North American F-51D Mustang with strengthened wings and additional underwing pylons for air-to-ground weapons.

During early 1961, Cessna began development of an armed variant of the T-37 to be used in the armament training role. A standard production T-37B was modified with a strengthened wing, and a weapons pylon was installed under each wing outboard of the main wheel wells. Additionally, provision was made for 65 gallon wingtip fuel tanks.

The aircraft was to be armed with two General Electric multi-purpose pods, each containing a .50 caliber machine gun with 200 rounds, two 2.75 inch folding fin rockets and four 3 or 25 pound practice bombs. Weapons aiming and delivery was accomplished using a K14C computing gunsight. Additionally, the aircraft was equipped with an AN/N-6 16MM gun camera for scoring purposes.

For the reconnaissance role, provisions were made in the fuselage to carry a KA-20 or KB-10A tactical reconnaissance camera or an optional HC-217 mapping camera (rarely, if ever, actually used). After successful testing, the armed T-37 was ordered into production under the designation T-37C.

With the armament option, the T-37C became an obvious candidate for conversion to the COIN role, although the aircraft gained firepower at the expense of performance. With the maximum takeoff weight increased by some 1,433 pounds (with no increase in engine power) maximum speed fell from 425 mph to 370 mph.

The T-37C was intended primarily as an armed trainer to be exported to smaller nations aligned with or friendly to the US. Mission range could be extended to more than 1,100 miles when the 65 gallon wingtip fuel tanks were carried. The fuel was transferred from the tip tanks to the wing tanks by inline booster pumps, utilizing the existing internal fuel system. Provision was made for jettisoning the tanks in case of an emergency.

As an armed trainer, the T-37C could carry a variety of armament, including gun and/or rocket pods, bombs (up to 500 pounds), and provision was made for carrying AIM-9 Sidewinder air-to-air missiles.

Cessna used a modified T-37B as the prototype for the T-37C weapons trainer. The T-37C featured a weapons pylon under each wing and optional 65 U.S. gallon wingtip tanks. The pods on the pylons are General Electric multi-purpose pods which carried a .50 caliber machine gun, 2.75 inch rockets and practice bombs.

Wing Pylon

T-37C

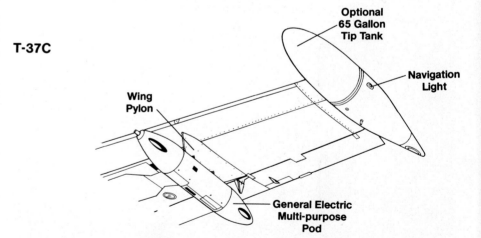

Optional 65 Gallon Tip Tank

Navigation Light

Wing Pylon

General Electric Multi-purpose Pod

The underwing weapons pylon on the T-37C could carry a variety of weapons such as this XM-157 seven shot 2.75 inch Folding Fin Aircraft Rocket (FFAR) pod. The pylon was stressed for loads up to 500 pounds.

This Cessna T-37C (66-13612) is fitted with the optional 65 gallon wingtip fuel tanks but is not fitted with the underwing weapons pylon. The inboard side of the tip tanks are painted in Flat Black to serve as anti-glare shields.

This Cessna T-37C (62-2497) was the 777th T-37 built and was later exported to the Portugese Air Force where it received the serial number 2426. The metal rail under the wing is the mounting bracket for the weapons pylon.

15

T-37 Exports

The T-37A and B were widely exported and the T-37C was designed and built with the export market in mind. Numerous T-37s were provided to friendly governments under the Military Assistance Program (MAP), while others were purchased by foreign countries directly from Cessna (with government approval).

These exports included the following:

The Brazilian Air Force bought sixty-five T-37Cs. During 1980, thirty were sold to South Korea. Twelve were later transferred to the Paraguayan Air Force during 1982.

The Burmese Air Force obtained twelve T-37Cs between 1971 and 1972.

Cambodia (Kampuchea) received four ex-USAF T-37Bs (60-0148, 0148, 0150, and 0159) in March of 1962. These aircraft arrived on board a USAF Douglas C-124B and, after being assembled, were test flown by a Cessna test pilot. By 1975 the T-37Bs had been reduced to hulks rotting alongside the runway at Pochentong Air Base.

The Chilean Air Force received a total of thirty-two T-37s: twenty T-37Bs and twelve T-37Cs. Most of these served with the air force training school, the *Escuela de Aviacion "Captain Avalos,"* at El Bosoque Air Base.

The Columbian Air Force took delivery of fourteen T-37s: four T-37Bs and ten T-37Cs. They were delivered during 1969 to the School of Military Aviation at Cali. Later the aircraft were transferred to the Combat Air Group at Barranquilla.

The Federal Republic of Germany (Luftwaffe) received forty-seven T-37s. These aircraft were retained in the U.S. and carried standard USAF markings. The aircraft were attached to the 80th Flight Training Wing at Williams AFB near Phoenix, Arizona and used for training German pilots who were to go on to the F-104 Starfighter. The German T-37s were all T-37Bs (66-7960 thru 8006).

The Greek Air Force (*Elliniki Aeroporia Royal Helenic Air Force*) took delivery of thirty-two T-37s of which eight were T-37Bs and twenty-four were T-37Cs. The aircraft were attached to the *361 Mira Ekpiteyseos* (Training Squadron), which is part of the 120th Air Training Wing at Kalamata and a component of the *Ethniki Aeroporia Acadymia* (National Air Academy).

Jordan (*Al Quwwat al Jawwiya al Malakiya al Urduniya*) received fifteen T-37. Nine aircraft were leased from the USAF during 1975, then purchased outright the following December. The remainder were operated on loan from the USAF.

South Korea (*Hankook Kong Goon*) originally received twenty-five T-37Cs and purchased another thirty from Brazil during 1980.

Pakistan (*Pakistan Fiza'ya*) obtained a total of sixty-three T-37s of which twenty-four were T-37Bs and thirty-nine were T-37Cs. Some of the T-37s are assigned to Nos 1 and 2 Basic Flying Training Squadrons of the PAF Air Academy at Risalpur.

The Peruvian Air Force took delivery of thirty-two T-37Bs, all of which now serve with Squadron 512 of Group 51 at Las Palnnas, which is part of the Officers School.

The Portugese Air Force had thirty T-37Cs. A number of these were attached to Pilot Squadron 102 at Sintra as part of Group 21. Other T-37s were assigned to the Wings of Portugal, the national aerobatic team and carried Red, White, and Green color scheme.

Thailand (Royal Thai Air Force) received ten T-37Bs and six T-37Cs for use at the Flying Training School at Kamphaeng Saen. The T-37Bs arrived in 1961 and the T-37C were received during 1970.

Turkey (*Turk Hava Kuvvetleri*) received fifty T-37Cs which were assigned to 122 *Filo* at Cigli.

The South Vietnamese Air Force (VNAF) received twenty-four T-37Bs which retained their USAF serials. These aircraft operated from Phan Rang after that base was turned over to the VNAF during 1971. T-37s were also used by the VNAF Air Training Center at Nha Trang.

A Brazilian Air Force officer conducts an acceptance flight of a new production T-37C at the Cessna factory on 7 January 1969. The rudder stripes are Green and Yellow and the aircraft carries the Brazilian star in four wing positions. Brazil was one of the first export customers for the T-37.

Five Cessna T-37Cs destined for the Brazilian Air Force prepare for their delivery flight on the Cessna flight line at Wichita, Kansas. Normally, aircrews from Brazil would travel to the Cessna facility, conduct the acceptance flights and then ferry the aircraft back to Brazil.

A Cessna T-37C (0882) of the Brazilian Air Force assigned to the *Academia de Forca Aerea* (AFA) or Air Force Academy at *Campo de Marte* during May of 1977. The aircraft had recently been repainted with Day Glo Orange nose, fuselage, tail and wing bands.

This Brazilian T-37C (0932) is assigned to the AFA (the Brazilian Air Force Academy). The Day Glo Red markings faded rapidly in the equatorial heat and humidity in Brazil. The rudder markings are Green and Yellow, with all numbers and lettering in Black. (Dan Hagedorn)

17

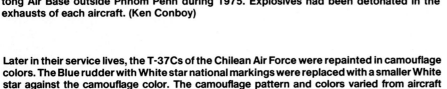

The Royal Cambodian Air Force received four T-37Cs under MAP, which retained their former USAF "Buzz" numbers. The aircraft were rendered useless by a sapper attack at Pochentong Air Base outside Phnom Penh during 1975. Explosives had been detonated in the exhausts of each aircraft. (Ken Conboy)

J-391 is a T-37C of the Chilean Air Force. The aircraft was exported to Chile under the Military Assistance Program (MAP) and was taken from the U.S. Air Force inventory. In fact, USAF markings are still faintly visible under the Chilean national insignia.

Later in their service lives, the T-37Cs of the Chilean Air Force were repainted in camouflage colors. The Blue rudder with White star national markings were replaced with a smaller White star against the camouflage color. The camouflage pattern and colors varied from aircraft to aircraft.

T-37Cs of the Columbian Air Force (*Fuerza Aerea Columbia*) on the ramp at the *Escuela Militar de Aviacion*. Over the years the FAC has lost two of the original ten T-37s delivered to accidents. The rudder striping (top-bottom) is Yellow, Blue and Red.

The third T-37C delivered to the Columbian Air Force (Fuerza Aerea Columbiana - FAC) was FAC-2103. Columbia took possession of the T-37s at Howard AFB, Canal Zone, Panama. FAC-2103 was part of a delivery that took place on 2 December 1969. (Dan Hagedorn)

An early T-37C (62-5973) of the Royal Helenic Air Force carries the same style markings as the USAF Air Training Command: Black buzz numbers and Day Glo Orange (or Red) panels on the nose, wings and tail.

This overall Natural Metal Cessna T-37C (69-7599) of the Pakistani Air Force has a Day Glo panel on the nose. The Pakistani national insignia is Dark Green and White and all numbers are in Black. (Charles Mayer)

19

This Cessna T-37C on the ramp at the Cessna facility is destined for the Peruvian Air Force (Fuerza Aerea Peru). The aircraft stenciling was in Spanish, not English. The rudder stripes are Red, White, Red and the aircraft number is in Black.

Eight T-37Cs for the Peruvian Air Force are parked alongside seven other T-37s on the Cessna flight line at Wichita International Airport. The Peruvian Air Force carries a roundel on the upper port wing and the aircraft serial number on the upper starboard wing in Black.

This Cessna T-37C (2415) of the Portguese Air Force carries the Red, White and Green markings of the Portguese Air Force Aerial Demonstration team — *Asas de Portugal* (Wings of Portugal).

Asas de Portugal operates eight T-37Cs and was formed during 1977 at Sintra Air Base. The team has flown hundreds of demonstrations throughout Europe, The only modification done to the aircraft was the installation of a smoke system and the isolation of one fuel cell to carry oil for the system.

Six T-37s parked on the flight line of an air base in Thailand. The aircraft carry Day Glo Orange panels with Natural Metal panels where the old USAF buzz numbers and serial numbers were removed (in preparation for application of Thai Air Force serials).

This T-37C carries full Royal Thai Air Force (RTAF) serials and aircraft side numbers. In the tropical climate of Thailand the Day Glo Orange high-visibility panels quickly faded out to patchy and almost Yellow color.

The dedication and blessing of a new Cessna T-37C of the Turkish Air Force at Cigli Air Base during March of 1964. The blessing includes the sacrifice of a lamb. The Turkish national insignia at this time consisted of a Red and White square (later changed to a Red/White/Red roundel).

21

YAT-37D/A-37A

During late 1962, the newly established Special Air Warfare Center at Eglin AFB, Florida, evaluated two T-37Cs for their possible use in the counterinsurgency (COIN) role. After completing the evaluation, the Air Force decided to develop an improved variant of the T-37C with a greater weapons load, increased range, higher thrust engines and better short field performance.

During 1963, Cessna received a contract from the Aeronautical Systems Division at Wright-Patterson AFB for two prototypes under the designation YAT-37D (Cessna Model 318D) for Category I, II and III evaluation. The YAT-37D would be flown in competition with the turboprop powered North American YAT-28E. Cessna was given only six months to deliver the first YAT-37D, despite the fact that the T-37 would require major redesign work that would double the aircraft's gross weight and that the aircraft would also require re-engining.

In the early stages of the development program, gross weight had increased from 6,600 pounds to some 8,700 pounds, while the aircraft retained the Continental J-69-T-25 engine. Cessna realized that this engine could not be modified to give the power needed, and to reach the target gross weight of 10,500 pounds an entirely new engine would be needed. As a result, the YAT-37D was fitted with two 2,400 lbst General Electric J85-J2/5 engines, more than doubling the available thrust.

Other major changes in the two YAT-37Ds (ex-T-37B 62-5950 and 5951) included strengthening the wings, installation of six underwing pylons for external stores (three on each wing), self-sealing fuel tanks, cockpit armor, a nose mounted General Electric GAU-2B/A 7.62MM Minigun with 1,500 rounds of ammunition, a Mark 20 Mod 4 gun sight, a gun camera mounted alongside the gun sight, larger wheels and tires for rough field operations, 95 gallon wing tip fuel tanks, and a special electronics package for communications, navigation and target acquisition. With all modifications completed, the first YAT-37D prototype made its first flight on 22 October 1963 under the control of Cessna test pilot James LeSueur.

Flight testing was conducted jointly by Cessna and USAF pilots from Edwards Air Force Base, California to accelerate the program and to begin the Category II evaluation as soon as possible. Additional tests at Edwards and at the Special Air Warfare Center, Eglin AFB, Florida were conducted during 1964 using the second prototype (62-5951).

While USAF interest in a COIN aircraft had diminished, the widening combat commitment in Vietnam, together with a higher-than-anticipated loss rate of Douglas A-1 Skyraiders, made it necessary to conduct a reappraisal of the various COIN programs. This reapprasial was aimed at finding a suitable aircraft to deploy to Vietnam to replace the aging A-1s. From its initial development trials, the YAT-37D had shown that it offered considerable advantages as a limited warfare close air support aircraft and light strike aircraft. The Air Force, however, decided that the only way to properly evaluate the aircraft would be under actual combat conditions in South East Asia.

As a result of this decision, the USAF placed a contract with Cessna for a preproduction evaluation batch of thirty-nine aircraft under the designation AT-37D (67-14504 through 14541). Shortly after the contract was let, the aircraft was redesignated as the A-37A. A number of these aircraft were to be deployed to Vietnam as part of the *Combat Dragon* program which was aimed at evaluating the aircraft in combat. At the same time, the second YAT-37D prototype was taken out of the Air Force museum, overhauled and put into a new test program under the designation YA-37A. During this overhaul, a fourth pylon was added under each wing to bring the YA-37 up to A-37A standards.

To speed up the *Combat Dragon* program, the thirty-nine A-37As were converted from standard T-37B airframes and differed only in small details from the YAT-37D prototypes. Gross weight of the A-37A had risen to 12,000 pounds which allowed for a maximum weapons load of some 4,700 pounds with a crew of two, or 4,855 pounds with a pilot only. Full dual controls were retained so that the A-37 could also be used for normal training. When not used for training, the second seat could be used by an observer.

In August of 1967, twenty-five of the thirty-nine A-37As were deployed to Vietnam and attached to the 604th Air Commando Squadron. During their first four months in Vietnam, the A-37As flew more than 5,000 sorties from Bien Hoa Air Base. They operated in six basic roles — close air support, helicopter escort, combat air patrol, armed reconnaissance, forward air control and night interdiction. Some 3,000 sorties were made by the A-37As in Vietnam without a single loss to enemy fire, although twenty-four aircraft suffered hits from Viet Cong gunners and two crashed in landing accidents.

One of the two YAT-37D prototypes on the ramp at Wright-Patterson Air Force Base. This aircraft carries six wing pylons loaded with six LAU-3A nineteen shot 2.75 inch rocket pods. The prototypes later added another wing pylon on each wing for a total of eight.

The YAT-37D (62-5950) was configured with a double launcher for the AIM-9 Sidewinder air-to-air missile on a single T-37C style wing pylon. Although tested and found to be feasible, the AIM-9 Sidewinder installation was not used on the A-37A in operations.

Wing Pylons

YAT-37D (Early)

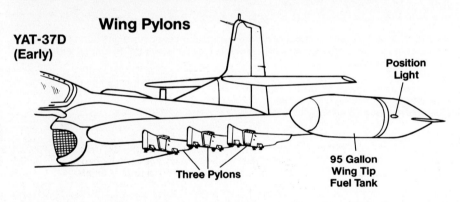

Position Light

Three Pylons

95 Gallon Wing Tip Fuel Tank

YAT-37D/A-37A

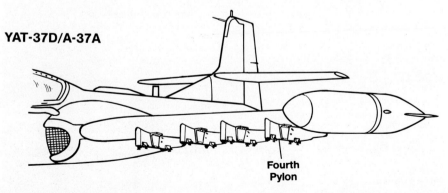

Fourth Pylon

One of the two YAT-37D (62-5950) prototypes demonstrates its power and maneuverability by looping with a full load on the underwing pylons. The YAT-37D carried a ninety-five gallon tip tank in place of the 65 gallon tank carried on the T-37C.

The second YAT-37D was the first to be fitted with four underwing weapons pylons. Later the first prototype was retrofitted with four pylons and this configuration was settled on for the production A-37A.

The YAT-37D underwent a number of different armament configurations during testing. For this test the aircraft is configured with a Multiple Ejection Rack (MER) loaded with five 500 pound WW II bombs.

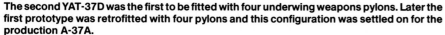

The second YAT-37D (62-5951) was configured with eight underwing pylons. During this test the aircraft was armed with eight napalm tanks. The aircraft could also carry similar fuel drop tanks, although tests revealed that fins were needed on drop tanks (and wingtip tanks) for better separation when being jettisoned.

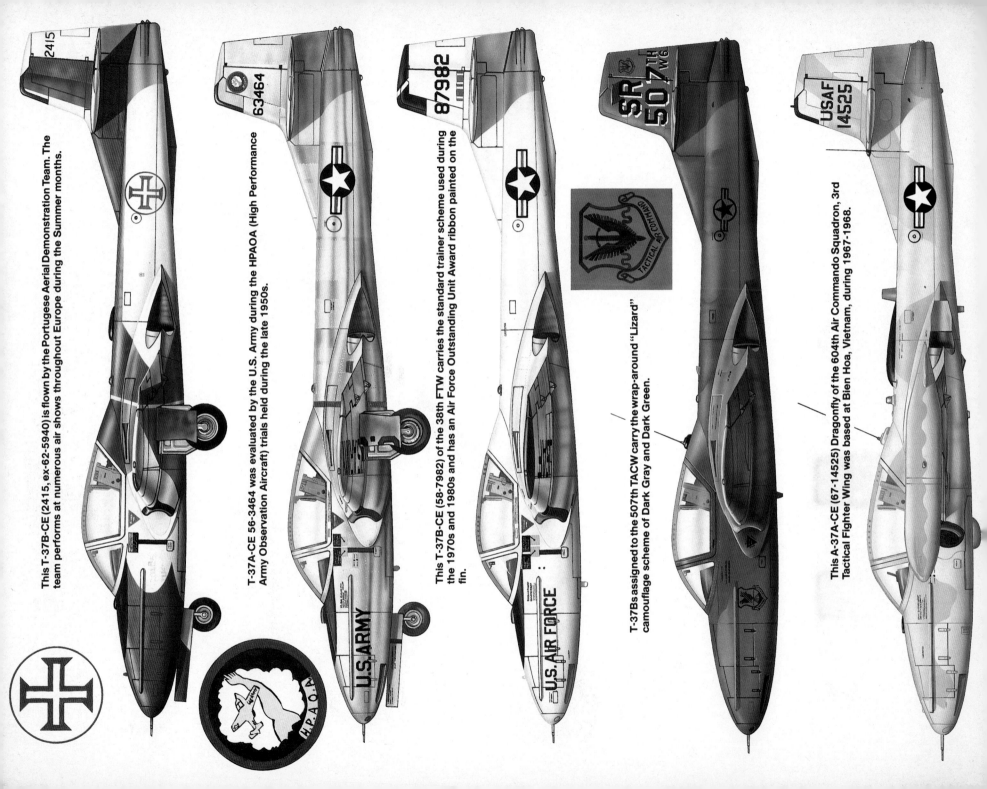

This T-37B-CE (2415, ex-62-5940) is flown by the Portugese Aerial Demonstration Team. The team performs at numerous air shows throughout Europe during the Summer months.

T-37A-CE 56-3464 was evaluated by the U.S. Army during the HPAOA (High Performance Army Observation Aircraft) trials held during the late 1950s.

This T-37B-CE (58-7982) of the 38th FTW carries the standard trainer scheme used during the 1970s and 1980s and has an Air Force Outstanding Unit Award ribbon painted on the fin.

T-37Bs assigned to the 507th TACW carry the wrap-around "Lizard" camouflage scheme of Dark Gray and Dark Green.

This A-37A-CE (67-14525) Dragonfly of the 604th Air Commando Squadron, 3rd Tactical Fighter Wing was based at Bien Hoa, Vietnam, during 1967-1968.

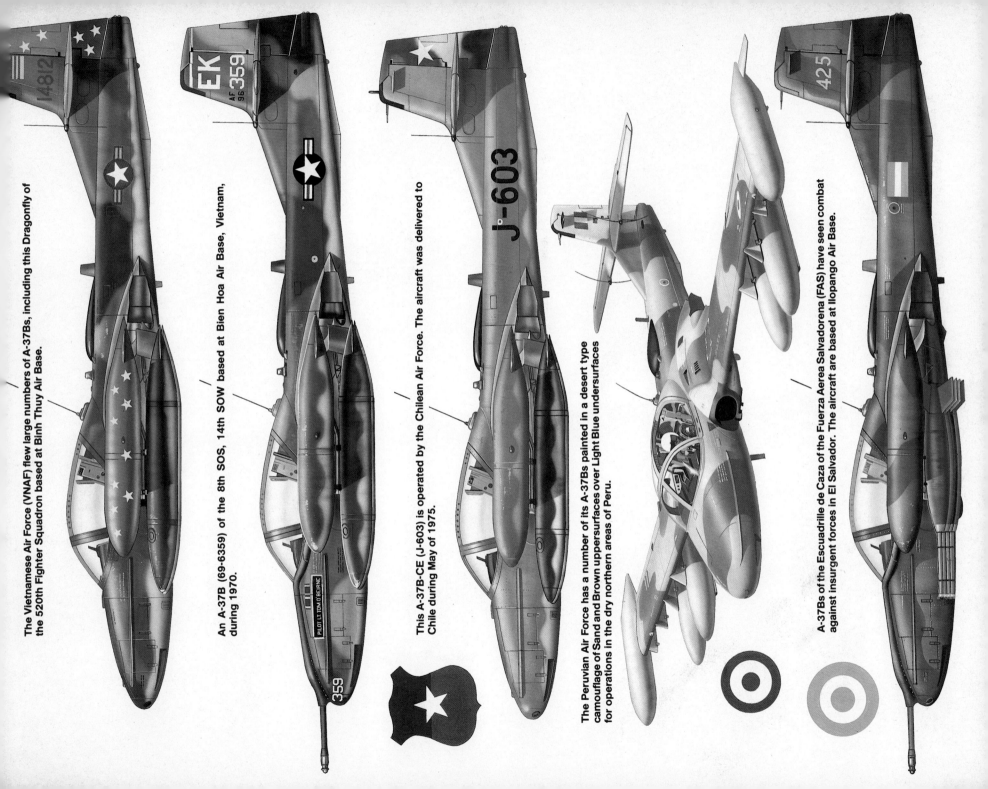

The Vietnamese Air Force (VNAF) flew large numbers of A-37Bs, including this Dragonfly of the 520th Fighter Squadron based at Binh Thuy Air Base.

An A-37B (69-6359) of the 8th SOS, 14th SOW based at Bien Hoa Air Base, Vietnam, during 1970.

This A-37B-CE (J-603) is operated by the Chilean Air Force. The aircraft was delivered to Chile during May of 1975.

The Peruvian Air Force has a number of its A-37Bs painted in a desert type camouflage of Sand and Brown uppersurfaces over Light Blue undersurfaces for operations in the dry northern areas of Peru.

A-37Bs of the Escuadrille de Caza of the Fuerza Aerea Salvadorena (FAS) have seen combat against insurgent forces in El Salvador. The aircraft are based at Ilopango Air Base.

The second YAT-37D (62-5951) salvos a full load of 2.75 inch rockets from one of the four nineteen shot LAU-32A rocket pods it is carrying. In addition to the LAU-32A pods, the aircraft is carrying a practice bomb carrier on the outboard pylon loaded with four twenty-five pound bombs.

One of the YAT-37D prototypes test fires the nose mounted General Electric GAU-2B/A 7.62ᴍᴍ Minigun. The ammunition bay had a capacity for 1,500 rounds of ammunition. The gun on the wing pylon is a .50 caliber M-3 machine gun pod.

Nose Development

T-37B

YAT-37D/A-37A

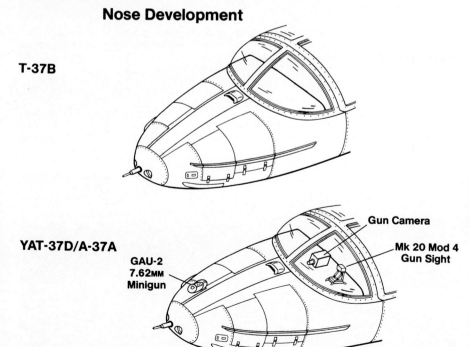

The gun bay on the A-37A was very large and easily accessible to ordnance personnel. The electrically driven General Electric GAU-2B/A 7.62ᴍᴍ Minigun fired at a rate of 3,000 rounds per minute and the gun bay had a capacity of 1,500 rounds of ammunition.

27

Ground crews perform minor maintenance on an A-37A in its revetment on a South Vietnamese air base during September of 1967. Its ease of maintenance was one of the strong points of the A-37. This aircraft was originally built as a T-37A and later converted to A-37A standards. (USAF)

This A-37A (67-14524) carried an experimental camouflage of overall Light Pale Blue. A modified version of this color scheme (with the addition of a Light Gray pattern) was adopted for some of the A-37s that deployed to Vietnam.

This A-37A (67-14525), parked in a blast revetment at Bien Hoa Air Base, Vietnam, was originally built as a T-37A (56-3471) then converted to A-37A standards. The aircraft is armed with two Mk 82 bombs, two fuel tanks, two napalm tanks and two SUU-14 bomblet dispensers.

The "Last Chance" area at Bien Hoa Air Base is where all ordinance was checked and safety pins were removed before taking off on a mission. These A-37As carry the Pale Blue and Light Gray experimental color scheme in use during January of 1968. (Author)

Three A-37As of the 604th SOS, 3rd Tactical Fighter Wing on the ramp at Bien Hoa Air Base during October of 1967 carry the Pale Blue camouflage, while the last two in the line have been repainted in the darker Southeast Asia camouflage. (Author)

A ground crewman directs the pilot of this A-37A (67-14511) of the 604th SOS to hold position in its revetment at Bien Hoa Air Base. The aircraft is armed with a mixed load of ordnance including low drag 500 pound bombs and a 7.62mm Minigun pod. (Aviation Week)

29

The White EK tail code identifies this A-37A as belonging to the 604th Special Operations Squadron (SOS), 3rd Tactical Fighter Wing (TFW) at Bien Hoa Air Base, South Vietnam. The 604th SOS was the only USAF unit to fly the A-37A on operations.

An A-37A fires 2.75 inch rockets at Viet Cong targets in South Vietnam. For ground attack missions, the A-37As were normally flown as single seat aircraft. Also, the aircraft normally carried underwing fuel tanks to increase their loiter time over target.

Three A-37As of Detachment 1, 3rd Tactical Fighter Wing lift off from the runway at Bien Hoa Air Base, South Vietnam during late 1967 or early 1968. All three aircraft are carrying fuel tanks on the inboard pylons and a variety of ordinance on the other pylons.

A-37B/OA-37B

While highly successful, the *Combat Dragon* program highlighted a number of problems in the A-37A, most notably in its restricted range/loiter time. Additionally, pilots reported that the aircraft had severe control loads when carrying weapons at normal weapons delivery speeds (approximately 400 knots). The lack of redundancy in the primary control runs was another concern. As a result of these reports, the Air Force ordered the A-37A to be modified to overcome these and other shortcomings under the designation A-37B (Cessna Model 318E).

Production orders for the A-37B were issued for fifty-seven aircraft, with this contract being increased to 127 within a short time. The initial A-37B contract (AF 3-3657-67-C-0825) was being negotiated at the time that the A-37A contract was officially awarded (August of 1966). The A-37Bs were, from the beginning, intended to serve as replacements for the Douglas A-1 Skyraiders of the South Vietnamese Air Force (VNAF). Cessna received its first $3.6 million contract for the A-37B on 23 January 1967, with deliveries due to begin during May of 1968. Since the A-37B was to be a new construction aircraft, Cessna incorporated a number of structural changes which further increased gross weight to 14,000 pounds.

These changes included an automatic de-icing system in the engine air inlet to prevent inlet icing. The system fed bleed hot air from the engine through the lips of the inlet. The instrument panel was redesigned to facilitate flying the aircraft from either seat and an automatic engine starting system was added.

The A-37B had a structural limit of 6 Gs as compared to 5 Gs for the A-37A. The A-37B also had an improved fatigue life with a design maximum of 4,000 hours (extensive testing has shown that this figure can be safely raised to some 7,000 hours). The maximum gross weight allowed is 15,000 pounds (after aerial refueling) with an empty weight of 5,873 pounds. The A-37B has a disposable load of 9,527 pounds including up to 5,880 pounds of external stores. The takeoff weight of the A-37B was nearly double that of the earlier T-37C.

The A-37B was equipped with an AN-6N-6 16MM gun camera mounted in the center of the nose in place of the camera carried alongside the gun sight on the A-37A. The 7.62MM GAU-2B/A Minigun installation is the same as on the A-37A, together with the 1,500 round ammunition drum. A selector switch in the cockpit allows the pilot to vary the rate of fire of the gun from 3,000 to 6,000 rounds per minute. To increase fire power, underwing gun pods were developed for the A-37B. The pods can carry either a 30MM DEFA-553 cannon firing at a rate of 1,350 rounds per minute or a 20MM GPU-2/A cannon firing at 750 to 1,500 rounds per minute. With 250 rounds, the DEFA pod weighs some 750 pounds, while the GPU-2/A pod with 300 rounds weighs 550 pounds. Besides these two pods, the A-37B can also carry the SUU-11/A 7.62MM Minigun pod.

The A-37B also had provision for inflight refueling by means of a fixed nose probe, which fed fuel into external piping installed around the base of the canopy, connecting into the internal fuel system over the air intakes. Additionally, the fuel system was modified with foam filled self sealing tanks to counter the threat of fire and explosion should the cell be hit by enemy fire. The A-37B is unusual in that it is the only USAF fixed wing combat aircraft to use the probe and drogue method of refueling.

The engine power of the A-37B was increased over the A-37A with 2,850 lbst General Electric J85-GE-17A engines replacing the earlier 2,400 lbst J85-J2/5 engines. Because of the single engine cruise techniques developed with the A-37A, the engines of the A-37B were canted outward and downward slightly to minimize the effects of asymmetry with the increase in thrust.

To counter pilot complaints about a lack of control redundancy, the A-37B was fitted with duplicated elevator controls, with the control runs being widely separated. Flak curtains of layered nylon armor were installed around the cockpit (retrofitted to earlier A-37As). One of the lessons learned with the A-37A in Southeast Asia was that the cockpit needed air conditioning and this was installed on the A-37B.

The electronics suite includes UHF and VHF/FM communications, IFF, TACAN and ADF equipment. A bullet fairing, holding a long flexible antenna (which extended above and below the fairing), was added to each horizontal stabilizer. The cockpit is equipped with Weber ejection seats which are armored for additional crew protection. A bird strike resistant windshield was added later (during 1970).

The high pressure tires used on the A-37A were replaced with high flotation tires which were somewhat larger. The A-37B landing gear had new axles and wheels. To accommodate the larger wheels and tires, the main gear doors were bulged and enlarged slightly. The vortex generators, forward of the ailerons on the A-37A, were deleted on the A-37B.

To house the larger engines, the A-37B has slightly deeper engine nacelles. Additionally, the pitot tube was relocated from the nose (A-37A and T-37) to a position on the upper fin leading edge. Control system changes were incorporated to lighten stick loads at high speeds. These changes included the installation of force sensitive boost tabs on the ailerons, supplemented by slot-lip spoilers. The spoilers are hydraulically activated slots in the upper wing which provide a boost to lateral control at high speeds.

On normal combat missions, the A-37B is flown from the port side seat. This position has a full range of flight instruments, the armament switchs and the gun sight. The starboard seat (second pilot or observer) is provided with basic instruments and equipment for training/back-up flight. Unusual for a modern military aircraft, the A-37B is not pressurized and as a result its operational ceiling is limited to 25,000 feet by USAF regulations.

The overall Natural Metal A-37B prototype parked on the Cessna flight line during September of 1967. The aircraft was undergoing company tests and has test instruments in place of the starboard pilot's seat.

Refueling tests were conducted with the prototype A-37B using a Boeing KC-97G tanker. Early underwing, pylon-mounted drop tanks carried no fins, but tests revealed that there were tank separation problems and fins were added. A total of eight wing drop tanks plus the tip tanks and increased internal fuel gave the A-37B a greatly improved range over the earlier A-37A.

Additional orders for fifty A-37Bs were issued during September of 1968, followed by additional batches which brought the total on order by September of 1969 to some 366 aircraft (valued at some $73 million). The South Vietnamese Air Force (VNAF) received their first group of sixty A-37Bs during 1968, with the first squadron to re-equip with the A-37B being the 524th Fighter Squadron. VNAF conversion to the A-37B was assisted by the USAF, which continued to operate the A-37A with the 604th Air Commando Squadron. This unit flew from Bien Hoa Air Base for some time after the end of the *Combat Dragon* program. The unit had logged its 10,000th combat sortie over Vietnam during May of 1968.

The A-37B performed well in the Vietnam conflict, obtaining a high degree of weapons delivery accuracy in daylight, clear weather missions. Of the 577 A-37Bs built, 254 were transferred to the VNAF. After North Vietnam's victory over the South Vietnamese during 1975, about half of these fell into communist hands. Others that escaped Vietnam were passed on by the USAF to nearby friendly countries, like Thailand.

Recently released information has surfaced concerning North Vietnamese operations with the ninety-five A-37Bs that were captured after the fall of South Vietnam. The North Vietnamese incorporated the A-37s into the Vietnamese People's Air Force, with a number of the aircraft being assigned to the newly formed 937th Regiment. The A-37Bs saw action against counter-revolutionary units operating in the South and along the Cambodian border.

When Vietnam invaded Cambodia on 24 December 1978, the A-37s were used against Khmer Rouge targets in Cambodia. At least two A-37 pilots were awarded the title "Hero of the People's Armed Forces" for actions in Cambodia and the unit received the "Angkor Medal," Cambodia's highest military award. Reportedly, all A-37s have since been withdrawn and replaced by Su-7 Fitters in the ground attack role.

A further 110 A-38Bs were produced after the Vietnam war for export under the Military Assistance Program (MAP). These have recently been joined by aircraft being retired from USAF service. Following the U.S. withdrawal from Southeast Asia, the A-37B was phased out of Tactical Air Command service and passed on to the Air Force Reserve and Air National Guard units. Between 1980 and 1982, at least 122 A-37Bs were redesignated as OA-37Bs to reflect their new role as Forward Air Control (FAC) aircraft. These aircraft have since been replaced in the FAC mission by the more powerful and heavily armed and armored Fairchild OA-10A Thunderbolt II.

This A-37B was tested with two DEFA-533 30mm cannon gun pods on the inboard pylons. The two cannons and the single fuselage mounted 7.62mm minigun combined to give this A-37B awesome firepower. However, the gun pods were not adopted in standard service.

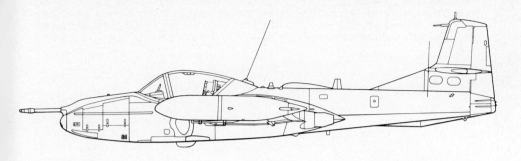

Specifications

Cessna A-37B Dragonfly

Wingspan .35 feet 10½ inches
Length . . . . .29 feet 3 inches (without probe)
Height . . . . .9 feet 3 inches
Empty Weight . . . . 6,211 pounds
Maximum Weight . . . . .15,000 pounds
Powerplant . . . . .Two 2,850 lbst General Electric
J85-17A engines.

Armament . . . . .One GAU-2B/A 7.62мм
Minigun and four underwing
ordnance pylons on each wing.

Performance
 Maximum Speed . . . . .507 mph
 Service ceiling . . . . .41,765 feet
 Range . . . . .920 miles
Crew . . . . .Two

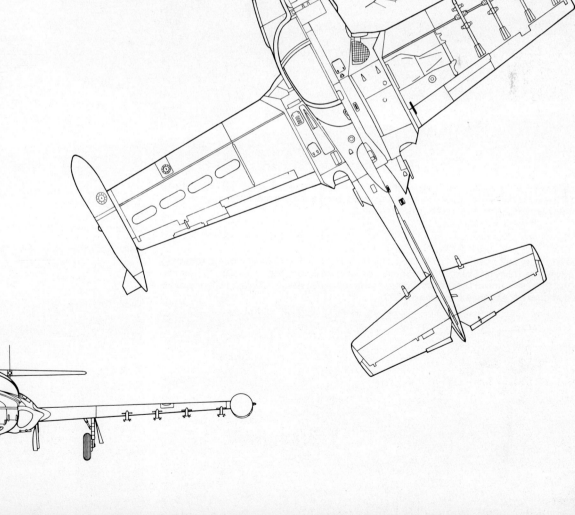

An A-37B (68-7930) on final approach for landing with the flaps, landing gear and speed brake down. The two thrust deflectors are deployed to slow the aircraft still further. With its wide track landing gear, the A-37B is easy to land.

An A-37B of the 8th SOS, 3rd Tactical Fighter Wing releases two Mk 82 high drag Snakeye 500 pound bombs on a suspected Viet Cong target. Although officially named the Dragonfly, the A-37 is more familiarly known as the "Super Tweet," a legacy of the unofficial name for its training ancestor, the T-37 "Tweety Bird."

The empty wing pylons of this 3rd Tactical Fighter Wing A-37B means that it was returning from a strike against Viet Cong/NVA targets. The inner two pylons are limited to 870 pounds, while the third and fourth pylons are limited to 600 pounds. The A-37B has a slightly more bulged engine nacelle than the earlier A-37A.

Four A-37Bs prepare to taxi out for another mission. The aircraft in the foreground with the EK tail codes are assigned to the 8th Special Operations Squadron, 14th Special Operations Wing. The second aircraft has a Red fin with a White border.

Fuselage Development

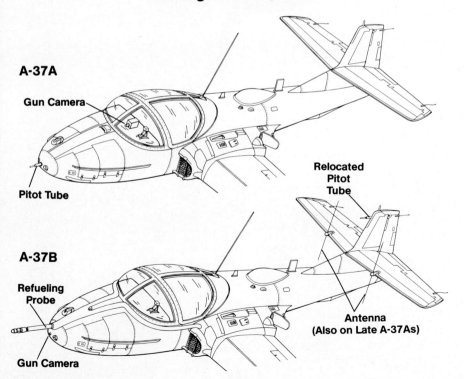

A-37A

Gun Camera

Pitot Tube

Relocated Pitot Tube

A-37B

Refueling Probe

Gun Camera

Antenna (Also on Late A-37As)

After the Vietnam War, A-37Bs were used for a variety of missions. This overall White A-37B (70-1307) was assigned to the Air Force Flight Test Center (AFFTC) at Edwards Air Force Base, California. The fin and horizontal stabilizer is Red. The aircraft carries a Red and White striped test probe.

This OA-37D Forward Air Control (FAC) aircraft is overall Gunship Gray. The bright spot on the nose is the aircraft's landing light. The OS tail code identifies the aircraft as being based at Osan, Korea.

A-37
FOD Screen

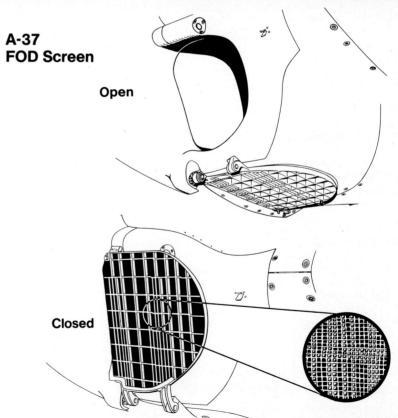

Open

Closed

Enlarged Detail of Wire Mesh

This A-37B (69-6371) is assigned to the 169th Tactical Air Support Squadron, 182nd Tactical Air Support Group based at Nellis Air Force Base, Nevada, during July of 1983. The aircraft carries Vietnam style camouflage. (Author)

A-37Bs in Foreign Service

The Cessna A-37B was widely exported under the Military Assistance Program to friendly foreign governments. The A-37B met the needs of these smaller air forces in that it was relatively inexpensive, economical to operate and it was easy to fly by young pilots with a more limited training background. Since it was not a highly technical aircraft, it was easy to maintain by young conscript maintenance personnel.

The largest export customer for the A-37B was the South Vietnamese Air Force (VNAF) which received some forty percent of the A-37Bs produced. Of the 577 A-37Bs built, the VNAF received sixty during 1969, 104 from 1970 to 1971 and ninety during 1972 (254 total). By the time the North Vietnamese overran South Vietnam in 1975, there were 187 remaining. Of these, ninety-two A-37Bs were recovered and ninety-five fell into communists hands.

Some of the former VNAF A-37Bs were given to other Asian countries: sixteen went to Thailand and twenty-seven went to the Republic of Korea Air Force (ROKAF). The rest were returned to the United States where they were turned over to Air National Guard and Reserve units (along with new production aircraft).

The rest of the A-37B were all exported to Central and South America. A number of these aircraft had a modified fueling system. The long aerial refueling probe was replaced with a short probe used as a high pressure single point fueling system. Other export A-37Bs had the nose probe deleted.

South America:

Peru (*Fuerza Aerea Peruana*) received thirty-six A-37Bs in two batches during 1974 and 1975. The Peruvian serial numbers were from 115 to 144 for the deliveries in 1974, and 145 to 156 for the deliveries during 1975. They are assigned to two squadrons of *Grupe* 7 at Piura. It was a Peruvian A-37B (156) that was the last A-37B built. When the aircraft rolled off the assembly line, it ended a production run that had started during 1955.

Chile (*Fuerza Aerea de Chile*) received sixteen A-37Bs during 1974 (serials J-600 to J-615). During 1975 Chile received an additional eighteen aircraft (serials J-616 to J-633) for a total of thirty-four. These operate with *Grupo* 1 of *I Brigada Aerea* at Iquique and *Grupo* 12 of *IV Brigada Aerea* at Punta Arenas.

Columbia (*Fuerza Aerea Colombiana*) received fourteen aircraft in two batches, ten during 1980, followed by an additional four aircraft (serials 2151 to 2174). These aircraft have been active in the anti-drug war in Columbia attacking known drug centers and processing areas. The aircraft are assigned to the 2 *Grupe* 21 at Apiay. Recently another twelve A-37Bs were reportedly delivered as part of an assistance package aimed at increasing pressure on the drug lords.

Ecuador (*Fuerza Aerea Equatiriana*) received twelve A-37Bs during 1975 (serials FAE374 to FAE385). They were delivered to *Escuadron de Combate 2112* Dragons at Taura, which is part of *Ala de Combate* 21.

Uraguay (*Fuerza Aerea Uraguaya*) received eight A-37Bs during 1975 (serials FAU270 and FAU277). These are operated by *Grupo de Aviaction* 2, which is part of *Brigada Aerea* 2 at Durazono.

Central America:

Honduras received six A-37Bs during 1974 (serials FAH1003 to FAH1008). These were followed by nine additional aircraft during 1975 (serials FAH1009 to FAH1017). The *Fuerza Aerea Hondurena* A-37s serve with *Escuadrilla de Ataque* at La Ceiba (Base Aerea Coronel Moncada).

Guatamala (*Fuerza Aerea Guatamalteca*) was the second country to take delivery of the A-37B, receiving eight during 1969 (various serials in the 416 to 428 range). During 1973 Guatamala received five additional A-37Bs (serials in the 432 to 448 range). The A-37Bs are flown by the *Escuadron Caza-Bonbardoo* based at San Jose although they were deployed to Flores during the late 1970s and early 1980s as part of the confrontation with Belize.

El Salvador (*Fuerza Aerea Salvadorian*) has recently received fifteen A-37Bs in three batches to reinforce the air force in its battle with leftist insurgents. These were delivered in batches of six, six, and three directly from the U.S. Air Force inventory. Early in 1991, three additional A-37Bs were delivered as attrition replacements.

This Cessna A-37 (68-7916) was assigned to the 516th Fighter Squadron based at Da Nang Air Base. After the American withdrawl from South Vietnam, the North introduced SA-7 ground-to-air missiles and the A-37s were prime targets as they flew low coming off their bomb runs.

Acquiring the Cessna A-37B Dragonfly was a major step forward in the modernization of the VNAF as the American involvement wound down. The A-37 carried a heavy load for its small size, and was a stable platform for weapons delivery. This A-37 was assigned to the 516th Fighter Squadron based at Binh Thuy.

The VNAF was the largest user of the A-37B with some 254 being delivered. This A-37B (68-10789) belonged to the 550th Fighter Squadron, 41st Tactical Wing during May of 1972. Some of these aircraft were later operated by the North Vietnamese over Cambodia.

CAPT Nguyen Thanh Trung (far left) was the lead pilot on the 28 April 1975 bombing raid on Tan Son Nhut AB outside Saigon. The North Vietnamese also claimed that he bombed the South Vietnamese Presidential Palace on 8 April 1975; however, this is unconfirmed. (Vietnam News Agency)

CAPT Nguyen Thanh Trung defected from the VNAF to the North Vietnamese in his A-37B (68-7955) during April of 1975. He then trained North Vietnamese MiG-17 pilots on the A-37 and they bombed Tan Son Nhut AB on 28 April 1975. (Vietnam News Agency)

FAP 119 is an A-37B of the Fuerza Aerea Peru (Peruvian Air Force). The A-37B had its national insignia applied later and the aircraft was delivered on 17 May 1975. The desert type camouflage indicated the aircraft was assigned to a base in Northern Peru.

The FAP is unusual in that it carries its insignia in the same style as the USAF. The Red/White/Red roundel is carried on the upper port wing and lower starboard wing, while the Black serial number is carried on the upper starboard wing and lower port wing.

Peruvian A-37Bs carry aerial refueling probes instead of the shorter single point fueling probes carried on other Latin American A-37s. The fin markings are Red, White, Red and the serial number under the fin flash is in Black. (via Nick Waters)

J-630 and J-629 belong to the Chilean Air Force and were part of the second batch of A-37Bs delivered to Chile during 1975. Chile received a total of thirty-four A-37Bs. (Hugh Muir)

This Cessna A-37B (serial J-600) of the Chilean Air Force (FAC) carries a Dark Green, Light Brown, and Light Tan uppersurface camouflage over Light Gray undersurfaces. These aircraft have a single point fueling probe in place of the aerial refueling probe carried on USAF A-37Bs.

J-633 is a A-37B of the Chilean Air Force and was the last of thirty-four A-37Bs delivered during 1974 and 1975. FAC serial numbers were J-600 to J-633. Later these aircraft were repainted in a much darker camouflage.

Refueling Probes

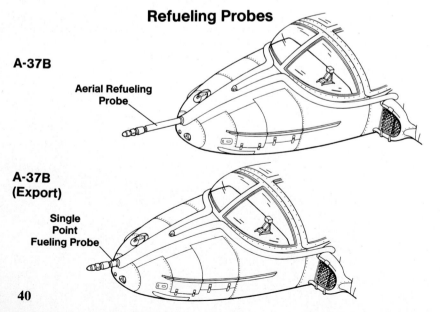

A-37B

Aerial Refueling Probe

A-37B (Export)

Single Point Fueling Probe

FAC 2158 was built for the Columbian Air Force (Fuerza Aerea Colombia FAC). This aircraft was the seventh (of fourteen) A-37Bs delivered to Columbia during November of 1980. The aircraft has a Red fin tip.

FAC-2151, an A-37B of the Columbian Air Force, carried a non-standard overall White color scheme during September of 1981. The aircraft carries full FAC rudder striping of Yellow, Blue, and Red. The aircraft serial number was repeated on the nose in Black.

Three Cessna A-37Bs are readied for delivery to the Ecuadorian Air Force (FAE) on the Cessna flight line at Wichita, Kansas. Each of the A-37Bs are loaded with four wing drop tanks for the long ferry flight to Ecuador. The fuselage markings are (top to bottom) Yellow, Blue, and Red.

The eight A-37Bs delivered to Uraguay during 1975 all carried the standard USAF South East Asia color scheme of Dark Green, Medium Green and Tan over Light Gray undersurfaces. FAU 275 was the sixth aircraft delivered and was an ex-USAF aircraft.

This Cessna A-37B (serial FAE-384) of the Ecuadorian Air Force (Fuerza Aerea Equadoriana) was delivered in standard USAF South East Asia colors. The A-37, being simple to maintain and operate, is widely operated in Central and South American.

These three Ecuadorian Air Force A-37Bs were delivered during 1975. The A-37 was well liked by most aircrews for its agility and load carrying capability. The aircraft are flown by the *Dragones* (Dragon) squadron based at Taura.

A robust and reliable aircraft, the A-37 has been exported to a number of smaller countries, including Uruguay. This A-37B, FAU 272, has all stenciling in Spanish. The A-37Bs replaced the Lockheed F-80C Shooting Star in the FAU's sole fighter squadron.

The FAU A-37Bs have been recently overhauled in the United States. As part of this overhaul, the aircraft received a new camouflage similar to the "Lizard" scheme carried by European based USAF OA-37Bs.

Weapons

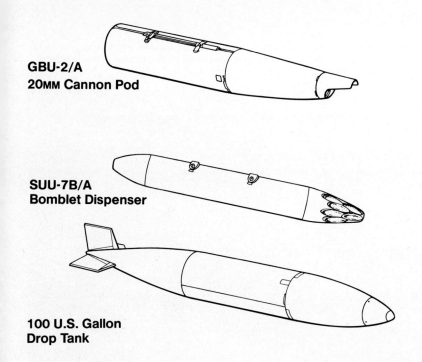

GBU-2/A
20ᴍᴍ Cannon Pod

SUU-7B/A
Bomblet Dispenser

100 U.S. Gallon
Drop Tank

LAU-32A 2.75 Inch
Rocket Pod

2.75 Inch Rocket

BLU1C/B
Finned Napalm Bomb

XM157 Seven Shot
Rocket Pod

Mk 81/82 Low Drag Bomb

SUU-14A Bomblet Dispenser

This A-37B was taken from USAF stocks, refurbished and exported to Honduras. The aircraft became FAH-1005 of the Hondurian Air Force during July of 1975. The aircraft carried the standard USAF SEA camouflage scheme.

The first two A-37Bs for Guatamala await their pilots for the delivery flight on 26 September 1974. The ferry flight was via Mexico and to comply with Mexican regulations, all armament was removed and the gunport was faired over. Lead weights were installed to compensate for loss of weight in the nose.

FAH-1003 was delivered to the Honduran Air Force (Fuerza Aerea Hondurian) during 1974. The A-37s were involved in flying ground support missions during border fighting with the Sandinista Army of Nicaragua.

Proposed T-37/A-37 Variants

Cessna, like other major aircraft manufacturers, discovered that there was a market for a business jet during the late 1950s. Since Cessna was fully involved with the T-37 at that time, the company decided to develop a civil variant based on the T-37 airframe. The result of this decision was the Cessna Model 407. The military also expressed an interest in a low-cost, high performance, multi-mission light jet. Cessna felt that the cost savings achieved though broadening a proven production aircraft, such as the T-37, was the best way to approach the problem (as did most other manufacturers).

The Cessna 407 was introduced during September of 1959 and differed from the T-37 in having a stretched airframe (two feet) housing a four-place cockpit. The aircraft was intended to serve both the military liaison role and as a corporate jet transport, using as many proven T-37 components as possible. The aircraft center section housed a four-place pressurized cabin with entry being made through a door on the starboard side. The rear passenger seats were removable to provide additional cargo space. In the event, Cessna could neither interest the military or civil market in the aircraft (although the prototype flew well). The military eventually purchased the North American T-39 Sabreliner (which utilized numerous parts from the F-86).

Cessna also adapted the T-37 to meet a Navy requirement for a tandem seating trainer under the Tandem Navy Trainer (TNT) proficiency aircraft program. Cessna's TNT candidate was basically a T-37 modified with a narrow fuselage housing a two seat tandem cockpit. The aircraft was to be powered by derated J85-4 engines. The Cessna entry was in competition with the North American T-2 Buckeye (which eventually won the contract).

Cessna also has proposed a T-37 replacement as part of the Next Generation Trainer (NGT) program. The entry was a T-37 modified with a T-tail and other improvements. In the event, this contract was eventually won by Fairchild with the T-46A (which was later cancelled).

As an offshoot of the TNT program for the U.S. Navy, Cessna proposed a tandem two-seat VTOL trainer using the TNT fuselage, with the addition of two large wing pods positioned about one third of the way down the wing. These pods were to house three small lift engines to give the aircraft vertical thrust. This project never progressed beyond the proposal stage.

Still utilizing the tandem TNT fuselage, Cessna proposed the AT-37E/STOL strike/recon aircraft for the low altitude close air support role mission. Modifications to the TNT included: higher thrust engines, wing tip extensions, increased chord flaps and larger thrust reversers. During this same time frame, Cessna proposed the same modifications except using a basic T-37 fuselage instead of the slender TNT fuselage. Neither proposal was accepted, although both were studied in great detail by the military.

While still trying to interest the U.S. Navy in a jet trainer, Cessna made another proposal for a Naval Instructional Trainer (NIT). This proficiency aircraft was basically an A-37 with J-85-4 engines, wing tip tanks, and fixed wing pods (similar to slipper tanks). This proposal proceeded almost to the sheet metal cutting stage before budget cuts and a diversion of funds for the Vietnam War caused the project to be cancelled.

An A-37 proposed derivative was the single seat A-37D which was an A-37B with more powerful engines, a center line rapid fire gun pod and the TNT slender fuselage. The rear seat was replaced with fuel and/or ammunition for the center line gun pod. Once again budgets cuts ended this project.

One of Cessna's most unique proposals was to replace the USAF Thunderbirds F-100 aircraft with Cessna T-37s. F-100s could only put on one show per day, were limited to relatively large airports and required expensive support teams. By using Cessna T-37s, the Thunderbirds could use smaller airports, put on more shows and attend other events that the USAF might be interested in supporting on a more frequent schedule. During 1962, however, there were no budget crunches and jet fuel was less than 10 cents per gallon, so the USAF stayed with the F-100.

Since Cessna had lots of experience in the attack aircraft business by the early 1970s, Cessna was included in the attack experimental (AX) program when the Air Force issued its Request For Proposals (RFP). Cessna presented their ideas and designs, but the Fairchild A-10 and the Northrop A-9 eventually won the AX competition for the fly-off, with the A-10 winning the production contracts.

During the late 1980s, plans for replacing the Cessna T-37 have had to be adjusted. The T-37's replacement was to have been the Fairchild T-46A, but the program did not go forward because of performance shortcomings, political considerations and a congressional order to the USAF to look again at all possible replacement options. One option was the Cessna T-48, which is a T-37B updated with new avonics, cockpit displays, a pressurized cockpit and a pair of 1,330 pound thrust Garrett F109-GA-100 turbofans engines (which powered the cancelled Fairchild T-46A).

The YT-48 prototype is scheduled to be produced from an existing T-37B airframe. Cessna is also offering a minimal update of the T-37B at a unit price of $300,000 each. The program would include strengthening the wing spars, tailplane, and the addition of other critical components to extend service life of the T-37 well into the next century.

The Cessna model 405 was a four-seat small jet transport proposed for the military. The four seat forward fuselage section was covered by a huge single-piece over head clamshell canopy. This design was not built and development was abandoned.

This Cessna model 407 prototype was modified with a large radar nose radome housing a weather radar. The aircraft reportedly flew well, but was underpowered for the additional weight of the four seat cabin.

The Cessna 407 prototype shares the company ramp with a T-37 of the Air Training Command. The Air Force tested the 407, but purchased the North American Sabreliner.

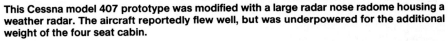

Cessna proposed a five-seat civilian/military liaison variant of the T-37 under the company designation Model 407A. It generated very little interest and was later abandoned, although the military prototype flew.

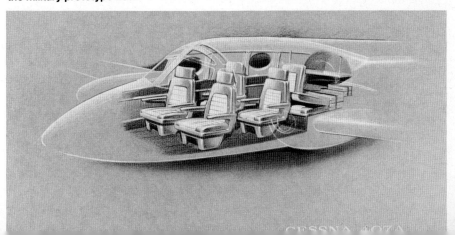

The competition for a T-37 replacement was known as the Next Generation Trainer program. Cessna's entry in that competition was a variant of the T-37 with larger engines and a T tail.

A company rendering of the proposed NGT (Next Generation Trainer) entry. The aircraft was basically a modernized T-37 with new engines, avionics and a "T" tail. The Fairchild XT-46 won the competition but was later cancelled.

Cessna proposed a tandem two-seat Vertical Take Off and Landing (VTOL) trainer for the USAF (based on an earlier Navy proposal). Although the design was abandoned, the Marines had expressed an interest in it as a trainer for the AV-8 Harrier.

47

TNT Trainer

NIT Trainer

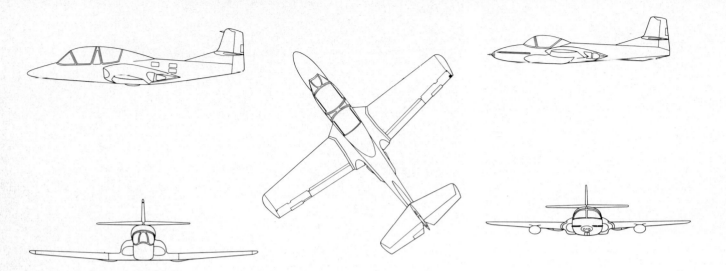

AT-37E/STOL (Tandem Seating)

AT-37E/STOL

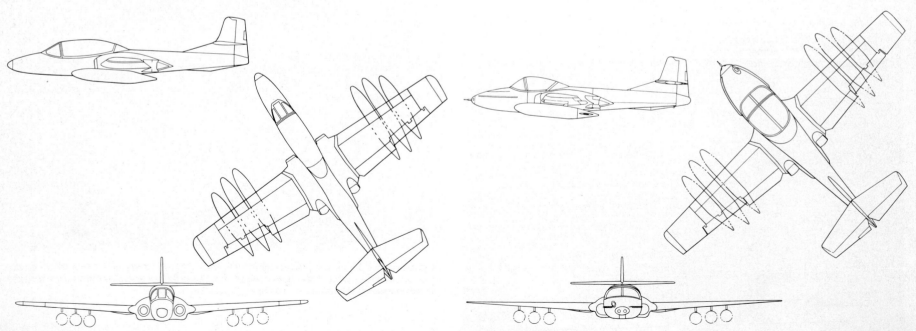

During October of 1962 the USAF Aerial Flight Demonstration Team the Thunderbirds, seriously considered the T-37 as its next demonstration aircraft. They decided, however, to stay with the F-100 till they later changed to the Nortrop T-38.

The U.S. Air Force announced a competition for a new attack aircraft to counter Soviet armor under the AX - Attack Experimental program. Cessna's experience with the A-37 made their AX proposal a serious contender; however, the Fairchild A-10 won the AX competition.

A-37D

The proposed A-37D had bigger more powerful engines, a nose mounted gun, a center line rapid fire gun pod and a single seat fuselage. Budget cuts of the late 1960s and early 1970s killed the project.

Aircraft Of The Vietnam War
from squadron/signal

1014

1065

1068

1070

1075

1077

1086

1087

1089

1091

1092